CM0079157

# A CENTURY of
# ROMFORD

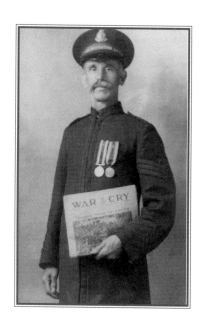

Stepladders, metal buckets, dustbins – this view along what was still a main road in the 1930s shows the market in full swing. The 86 bus ran through the market to Brentwood.

# A CENTURY of ROMFORD

BRIAN EVANS

SUTTON PUBLISHING

First published in 1999 by Sutton Publishing Limited

This new paperback edition first published in 2007 by
Sutton Publishing, an imprint of NPI Media Group
Cirencester Road · Chalford · Stroud · Gloucestershire · GL6 8PE

Copyright © Brian Evans, 1999, 2007
Copyright © 'Britain: A Century of Change', Roger Hudson, 1999, 2007

All rights reserved. No part of this publication may be reproduced, stored in a retrieval system, or transmitted, in any form or by any means, electronic, mechanical, photocopying, recording or otherwise, without the prior permission of the publisher and copyright holder.

Brian Evans has asserted the moral right to be identified as the author of this work.

British Library Cataloguing in Publication Data
A catalogue record for this book is available from the British Library.

ISBN 978-0-7509-4939-2

*Front endpaper*: The Romford market scene between the two world wars of the century remains captured forever in this charming lithograph by Dorothy Paton. The artist is working with the Laurie Hall behind her at the east end of the market plain.
*Back endpaper*: Romford market on a quiet day, *c.* 1965, provides a defining view of the town in the twentieth century as remembered by thousands of older Romfordians. This in spite of the fact that the Laurie Hall, its structure much battered in its latter days, was demolished approximately thirty years ago.
*Half title page*: Salvation Army soldiers would make their way from pub to pub, throughout the town, selling copies of *War Cry*. Though some customers would make slighting remarks, others respected the soldiers, male and female, for the impact they made on the poverty-stricken areas of the town in the first half of the century.
*Title page*: Still described as the new Post Office in South Street, the building – now a place of refreshment and entertainment known as Brannigans and much altered – was, in about 1912, flanked on the left by the Congregational Church and on the right by a front garden with trees, behind which lay a doctor's house.

Typeset in Photina.
Typesetting and origination by
Sutton Publishing.
Printed and bound in England.

# Contents

The top part of Junction Road leading to Main Road was still only a narrow footpath prior to these houses being built. The plaque commemorating the end of Queen Victoria's reign (1837–1901) is an interesting survival. Earlier plaques mark houses built in 1887 and 1897 during Victoria's golden and diamond jubilees. The plaques were made by Broadbent and Stevens of Leicester and were made in several potteries in that county – the firm being, at the time, one of the largest builders' merchants in the country.

# Britain: A Century of Change

Children gathered around an early wireless set in the 1920s. The speed and forms of communication were to change dramatically as the century advanced. (*Barnaby's Picture Library*)

The delirious rejoicing at the news of the Relief of Mafeking, during the Boer War in May 1900, is a colourful historical moment. But, in retrospect, the introduction that year of the first motor bus was rather more important, signalling another major adjustment to town life. In the previous 60 years railway stations, post-and-telegraph offices, police and fire stations, gas works and gasometers, new livestock markets and covered markets, schools, churches, football grounds, hospitals and asylums, water pumping stations and sewerage plants had totally altered the urban scene, as the country's population tripled and over 70 per cent were born in or moved to the towns.

When Queen Victoria died in 1901, she was measured for her coffin by her grandson Kaiser Wilhelm, the London prostitutes put on black mourning and the blinds came down in the villas and terraces spreading out from the old town centres. These centres were reachable by train and tram, by the new bicycles and still newer motor cars, con-nected by the new telephone, and lit by gas or even electricity. The shops may have been full of British-made cotton and woollen clothing but the grocers and butchers were selling cheap Danish bacon, Argentinian beef, Australasian mutton, tinned or dried fish and fruit from Canada, California and South Africa. Most of these goods were carried in British-built-and-crewed ships, burning Welsh steam coal.

As the first decade moved on, the Open Spaces Act meant more parks, bowling greens and cricket pitches. The first state pensions came in, together with higher taxation and death duties. These were raised mostly to pay for the new Dreadnought battleships needed to maintain naval superiority over Germany, and deter them from war. But the deterrent did not work. The First World War transformed the place of women, as they took over many men's jobs. Its other legacies were the war memorials which joined the statues of Victorian worthies in main squares round the land. After 1918 death duties bit even harder and a quarter of England changed hands in a few years.

Women working as porters on the Great Western Railway, Paddington, *c.* 1917. (*W.L. Kenning/ Adrian Vaughan Collection*)

The multiple shop – the chain store – appeared in the high street: Sainsburys, Maypole, Lipton's, Home & Colonial, the Fifty Shilling Tailor, Burton, Boots, W.H. Smith. The shopper was spoilt for choice, attracted by the brash fascias and advertising hoardings for national brands like Bovril, Pears Soap, and Ovaltine. Many new buildings began to be seen, such as garages, motor showrooms, picture palaces (cinemas), 'palais de dance', and the bow-windowed, pebble-dashed, tile-hung, half-timbered houses that were built as ribbon-development along the roads and new bypasses or on the new estates nudging the green belts.

During the 1920s cars became more reliable and sophisticated as well as commonplace, with developments like the electric self-starter making them easier for women to drive. Who wanted to turn a crank handle in the new short skirt? This was, indeed, the electric age as much as the motor era. Trolley buses, electric trams and trains extended mass transport and electric light replaced gas in the street and the home, which itself was groomed by the vacuum cleaner.

A major jolt to the march onward and upward was administered by the Great Depression of the early 1930s. The older British industries – textiles, shipbuilding, iron, steel, coal – were already under pressure from foreign competition when this worldwide slump arrived, cutting exports by half in two years and producing 3 million unemployed (and still rising) by 1932. Luckily there were new diversions to alleviate the misery. The 'talkies' arrived in the cinemas; more and more radios and gramophones were to be found in people's homes; there were new women's magazines, with fashion, cookery tips and problem pages; football pools; the flying feats of women pilots like Amy Johnson; the Loch Ness Monster; cheap chocolate and the drama of Edward VIII's abdication.

Father and child cycling past Buckingham Palace on VE Day, 8 May 1945. (*Hulton Getty Picture Collection*)

Things were looking up again by 1936 and unemployment was down to 2 million. New light industry was booming in the Home Counties as factories struggled to keep up with the demand for radios, radiograms, cars and electronic goods including the first television sets. The threat from Hitler's Germany meant rearmament, particularly of the airforce, which stimulated aircraft and aero engine firms. If you were lucky and lived in the south, there was good money to be earned. A semi-detached house cost £450, a Morris Cowley £150. People may have smoked like chimneys but life expectancy, since 1918, was up by 15 years while the birth rate had almost halved. The fifty-four hour week was down to forty-eight hours and there were 9 million radio licences by 1939.

In some ways it is the little memories that seem to linger longest from the Second World War: the kerbs painted white to show up in the blackout, the rattle of ack-ack shrapnel on roof tiles, sparrows killed

A family gathered
around their
television set in
the 1950s. (*Hulton
Getty Picture
Collection*)

by bomb blast, painting your legs brown and then adding a black seam
down the back to simulate stockings. The biggest damage, apart from
London, was in the south-west (Plymouth, Bristol) and the Midlands
(Coventry, Birmingham). Postwar reconstruction was rooted in the
Beveridge Report which set out the expectations for the Welfare State.
This, together with the nationalisation of the Bank of England, coal,
gas, electricity and the railways, formed the programme of the Labour
government in 1945. At this time the USA was calling in its debts and
Britain was beggared by the war, yet still administering its Empire.

Times were hard in the late 1940s, with rationing even more stringent
than during the war. Yet this was, as has been said, 'an innocent and
well-behaved era'. The first let-up came in 1951 with the Festival of
Britain and then there was another fillip in 1953 from the Coronation,
which incidentally gave a huge boost to the spread of TV. By 1954 leisure
motoring had been resumed but the Comet – Britain's best hope for

taking on the American aviation industry – suffered a series of mysterious crashes. The Suez debacle of 1956 was followed by an acceleration in the withdrawal from Empire, which had begun in 1947 with the Independence of India. Consumerism was truly born with the advent of commercial TV and most homes soon boasted washing machines, fridges, electric irons and fires.

The *Lady Chatterley* obscenity trial in 1960 was something of a straw in the wind for what was to follow in that decade. A collective loss of inhibition seemed to sweep the land, as stately home owners opened up, the Beatles and the Rolling Stones transformed popular music, and retailing, cinema and the theatre were revolutionised. Designers, hairdressers, photographers and models moved into places vacated by an Establishment put to flight by the new breed of satirists spawned by *Beyond the Fringe* and *Private Eye*.

In the 1970s Britain seems to have suffered a prolonged hangover after the excesses of the previous decade. Ulster, inflation and union troubles were not made up for by entry into the EEC, North Sea Oil, Women's Lib or, indeed, Punk Rock. Mrs Thatcher applied the corrective in the 1980s, as the country moved more and more from its old manufacturing base over to providing services, consulting, advertising, and expertise in the 'invisible' market of high finance or in IT. Britain entertained the world with *Cats*, *Phantom of the Opera*, *Four Weddings and a Funeral*, *The Full Monty*, *Mr Bean* and the *Teletubbies*.

The post-1945 townscape has seen changes to match those in the worlds of work, entertainment and politics. In 1956 the Clean Air Act served notice on smogs and pea-souper fogs, smuts and blackened buildings, forcing people to stop burning coal and go over to smokeless sources of heat and energy. In the same decade some of the best urban building took place in the 'new towns' like Basildon, Crawley, Stevenage and Harlow. Elsewhere open warfare was declared on slums and what was labelled inadequate, cramped, back-to-back, two-up, two-down, housing. The new 'machine for living in' was a flat in a high-rise block. The architects and planners who promoted these were in league with the traffic engineers, determined to keep the motor car moving whatever the price in multi-storey car parks, meters, traffic wardens and ring roads.

Carnaby Street in the 1960s. (*Barnaby's Picture Library*)

The Millennium Dome at Greenwich, 1999. (*Michael Durnan/Barnaby's Picture Library*)

The old pollutant, coal smoke, was replaced by petrol and diesel exhaust, and traffic noise. Even in the back garden it was hard to find peace as motor mowers, then leaf blowers and strimmers made themselves heard, and the neighbours let you share their choice of music from their powerful new amplifiers, whether you wanted to or not. Fast food was no longer only a pork pie in a pub or fish-and-chips. There were Indian curry houses, Chinese take-aways and American-style hamburgers, while the drinker could get away from beer in a wine bar. Under the impact of television the big Gaumonts and Odeons closed or were rebuilt as multi-screen cinemas, while the palais de dance gave way to discos and clubs.

From the late 1960s the introduction of listed buildings and conservation areas, together with the growth of preservation societies, put a brake on 'comprehensive redevelopment'. Now the new risk at the end of the 1990s is that town centres may die, as shoppers are attracted to the edge-of-town supermarkets surrounded by parking space, where much more than food and groceries can be bought. The ease of the one-stop shop represents the latest challenge to the good health of our towns. But with care, ingenuity and a determination to keep control of our environment, this challenge can be met.

# Romford: An Introduction

In 1900 Romford was a quieter town, that is if you avoided Wednesday – Market Day. Thursday half-day closing was a quiet time: it seems strange today that major businesses should have shut down at 1 p.m. in midweek. But this practice continued until well after the Second World War, gradually fading away as ever fewer businesses observed it. An interesting echo of those earlier days of the twentieth century is that until quite recently Thursday could sometimes still be an extremely quiet day for business – even though shops now stay open.

Of the other louder sounds that sometimes broke into the normally quite background level, various military and civil bands were welcomed perhaps for the excitement they added to a world without radio and television, though by 1913 silent films had arrived in Romford. The bands would parade through the town on special occasions or perform in one of the auditoriums then available – the Corn Exchange in the High Street was used for this purpose. There was also a bandstand provided in Raphael Park after its opening in the first decade of the century.

A new noise came with the arrival of the first petrol bus services in Romford. This took place without any of the vociferous opposition that had faced the proposals for tramway operation. The omnibus of course was much more flexible in negotiating the then narrow precincts of the town and it did not require the tearing up of the roadway in order to lay down its line of route. The London General Omnibus Company, founded in Central London in the mid-nineteenth century, decided to run a route from Burdett Road (for Mile End Station) to Romford market. This commenced on the 9 September 1912. For the first time Romford was to witness the roaring, juddering and spluttering of the 'B' type omnibuses. Their progress over the market cobbles and other **difficult road** surfaces,

Mashiter's Chase which later became Junction Road (top end) as the houses began to be built early in the century – this western side, however, was not built on until later.

13

with their solid tyres and imperfect springing, was something to be experienced.

The Great Eastern Railway was drawn into the project for a Garden Suburb at Gidea Park when, in September 1909, Herbert Henry Raphael paid a deposit of £500 to the G.E.R. under an agreement thought to relate to the building of a station to serve this new model estate. A clear-thinking individual, Raphael had seen the incalculable advantage a railway station situated nearby would confer on the success or otherwise of the undertaking (Gidea Park Ltd) of which he was Chairman. The directors urgently took steps to purchase the strip of land known as the Balgores Estate situated between the railway line and the hamlet of Hare Street, thus gaining control of the access route to the railway from the proposed estate, north of the main road. Squirrels Heath and Gidea Park station as it was first called was open in plenty of time to serve the houses then being constructed in the Garden Suburb. The date was 1 December 1910. It was of course well placed to pick up traffic from earlier housing development, east of Romford. The G.E.R. also had their sights on commuters from the recently developed Emerson Park Estate. The G.E.R.'s rival, the London Tilbury and Southend Railway, had stolen a march on it by opening a station at Butts Green (Emerson Park Halt) which was drawing off traffic to London through the one-stop connection at Upminster. As it happened the year of the planned 'House and Cottage Exhibition' at Gidea Park was to be the Coronation Year of George V and this gave a tremendous boost to the estate which was to be open to the public and potential purchasers from June to September, 1911.

What a surprise the outbreak of the First World War caused people in Romford and neighbourhood. Many men, who had for years enjoyed companionship and military training in the weekly and weekend drills of their local Volunteer Battalions, suddenly found that they had a real conflict in which to test their skills. As in most wars, there was plenty of initial chaos. Romford and Hornchurch men who volunteered to join up locally or in London were often despatched to training camps in other parts of the country. Conversely other potential soldiers from all over Britain found themselves part of a large force billeted in local schools.

The early days of radio (then known as the wireless) in the 1920s were spent trying to tune in and hold a crystal known as 'cats whisker' in position, so as to receive the transmissions which were at first broadcast for only a few hours a day. Just walking across the room could make the whisker jump and lose the sound. Later more up to date wireless sets with permanent reception were made but ran on a heavy battery filled with acid – the accumulator – which was attached to them. These had to be taken to a garage or other depot to be recharged, or exchanged as charging took some time. Monday and Tuesday were non-listening days in most families as the battery was in the depot. Often it would

14

be left till pay day on Friday or Saturday – when there was money and leisure available. Accumulators were still used after the Second World War as many homes were on gas and had no electricity or, where it did exist, there were only a few precious points to plug in appliances of one kind or another. Electric irons were often plugged in to a ceiling lampholder for this reason! In Romford there were a number of radio dealers from the 1920s onwards – as radio became more popular the different models updated yearly were advertised everywhere and there were scores of wholly British manufacturers of wireless sets – Ekco, Pye, Ferguson, Lissen, Brownie, Celestion and so on.

The scene in South Street, viewed from the railway bridge. Here in the early 1900s there was time for quiet contemplation. On the left is the Star Inn where a quick drink before catching the train was a policy of some Romfordians. Beyond was a plant nursery with a green plot beside a little shop. In the left distance rears the bulk of the old police station and magistrates' court. On the right there is a vacant plot and then W. Muskett's grocery, some other shops with offices above, including a servants' registry and further on is the County Court, with front gardens of private houses reaching towards Western Road.

One of the main radio stores in Romford was Silcocks of 55/58 High Street and 20 South Street who advertised in 1938 that they were dealers for Murphy, Marconiphone, Bush and Phillips radios. They were also beginning to sell a few television sets to the more wealthy local residents – these had incredibly small screens compared with today's models and were set in large consoles. Smarts Radio shop at 2a/2b Quadrant Arcade were promoting Ultra radio sets – 'The best value for money in 1937 is the Ultra 115,7 Stage Superhet, All Wave, Stations Named, A.C. Mains set at 10½ Guineas outright or 3 Shillings weekly hire purchase'.

From 1940, in the Second World War, the civilians of Romford were sometimes as involved with the dangers of warfare as the soldiers at the front. I well remember the trials of air-raid shelters as a very young child. The Anderson shelters outside in the garden filled with water in many locations including most located south of Main Road and London Road, Romford. Our family of three were lucky to have a cellar under our house which remained dry. When the air-raid sirens wailed we usually took shelter on the steps down to this. The staircase up to the first floor provided a protective ceiling above us as we listened to the drone of aircraft and the crump of bombs falling usually in the distance but sometimes too near and loud for comfort. The indoor Morrison shelter was a steel mesh box which could be covered and used as a table by day or would fit under the old-fashioned large wooden tables of which there were still many examples around. Of course these did not help if a bomb fell directly on top of them – although there were examples of incredible escapes from death by people in shelters, sometimes others were killed inside them.

Miss P. Corbell of Romford survived the war to record her memories of it and has this to say about the experience: 'War came and the Battle of Britain (in 1940). Being so near the aerodrome at Hornchurch we saw the fighters go up when the siren sounded and saw the dog fights in the sky when the planes came across the Channel to raid London. We saw the barrage balloons like big silver whales go up all round London to trap them. But our fighters were quicker and many turned and fled. One plane crashed in the fields at Stapleford, which caused quite a stir.

But the Night Raids that followed were worse, all night long we would hear the enemy bombers coming and going – with loud explosions when the bombs dropped. Our homes all had black-out over the windows, so no lights to warn them or show the way.

We had many bombs fall round us, one nearly fell on a shelter full of people but luckily it missed by a few feet and no-one was killed. The worst was a land mine in Essex Road, bringing down fifty houses and killing and injuring many. So day by day we carried on as usual. We went to school or work, never knowing if we would see each other again. But we didn't feel we would lose the War.'

The arrival of VE (Victory in Europe) Day brought people out on the streets and into the parks to celebrate. Many people travelled up to London, where the celebrations were bigger of course. It had to be admitted that returning service people arriving in our area discovered they had often been better off in the services – it was known as 'The Price of Peace'. While everybody in Romford were happy that the war was over and the dark shadow of aerial bombardment had lifted they soon began to realise that Britain was now engaged in a second battle – one to make ends meet and beat the shortages. Nearly all consumer items were in short supply – clothing, food, beer, cigarettes, petrol, cosmetics and houses. Part of the reason for this situation was that many factories had been turned over to war production for the duration, there was a shortage of materials world-wide and Britain had bankrupted herself over the cost of fighting the war. The standard of living was not high therefore – even before the war many of the items we cheerfully expect today were non-existent in the cost-conscious homes of many ordinary local citizens. Homes were rarely redecorated, thousands lacked basic amenities, families and individuals rarely ate out or brought home 'fast-food' apart that is from 'fish and chips' which was a truly economic meal and had always been. Yet many thousands could not afford even this. At the end of the war, however, some returnees and civilians had nest-eggs, not having been able to spend much of their income in war conditions. There also appeared, as always in times of shortage, flourishing 'black marketeers' who could obtain almost anything for a price.

In Romford after the Second World War, in spite of the shortage of everything, there occurred a kind of hiatus or interval where there was a rerun of pre-war interests. For instance the cinemas were madly popular

– there, in the American films, you could get a glimpse of a more luxurious lifestyle. In spite of the runaway housing developments between the First and Second World Wars, a large proportion of the local population lived in unimproved properties dating back to the 1900s and before. Domestic appliances in these Victorian and Edwardian homes were extremely rare. The better-off residents of course sometimes owned a vacuum cleaner, a pre-war console TV with its tiny screen, an electric cooker and kettle and electric lighting. There were very few houses with central heating – most of these would work from a solid fuel boiler which took up a large amount of room and circulated hot water via large circumference pipes which would not have looked out of place in a factory. Cinema-goers goggled at their local screens which showed opulent US homes fitted out with refrigerators, washing machines, dishwashers and food-mixers among other labour-savers and also featured bright-coloured furnishings, curtains, carpets and paintwork. In film locations such as California cinema audiences stared in disbelief at patios, loungers, barbecues and the joys of outdoor relaxation. The average Romfordian then returned home from the Rex, the Gaumont, the Odeon, the Vogue and contemplated his or her own, usually rather damp, residence which in some cases might have a scullery rather than a kitchen, a gas or coal-fired boiler to wash clothes in and a meat-safe in a cool alcove (a cupboard with perforated wire mesh windows) rather than a fridge. Before the Coronation in 1953 most people had a radio rather than a TV – the programmes on which were avidly listened to in the evenings, by a family who grouped themselves round it in the typical small and intimate living room. Mum would often be darning various socks and clothes for the umpteenth time, dad might be resting his feet in the water-filled enamelled tin bowl on the floor. Later dad would get out his shoe-repairing last and fit new leather/rubber soles or tip-protectors (Blakeys) with glue and small tacks if necessary. Plastic bowls and utensils were only just becoming available – from war factories which had previously turned out cockpit hods and suchlike made out of the new plastics. Such factories were beginning to produce consumer items in these materials for the first time. In pre-war days the older plastics, casein and bakelite had been used in only limited applications such as ashtrays, bus or coach fittings and as decorative additions to penknives and small articles, like razors. The pace of change and the expectation of an enhanced lifestyle had still not taken hold and many people, trained in war economy and on small budgets, conserved rather than bought new items. Professional conversion services were still in short supply, so many houses were still lit by the old gas-mantle lighting with the solid pipes projecting from the ceiling or wall into the light holder. Consumerism and economic boom were still in the future.

As the austerity of wartime began to be relaxed in the late 1940s and early 1950s a small hint of the later consumer boom started to stimulate Romford's economy.

With the end of rationing Romfordians could at last feast their eyes on new products in shop windows and stores. Most memorable was the end of chocolate/sweet rationing when shops were overwhelmed by a demand for chocolate bars and other types of confectionery that had been absent since the beginning of the war.

Record and music shops began to attract a new generation and American styles and artists were much favoured and copied. This interest in music and style, together with full employment, led to young people becoming for the first time an important part of the consumer market. Eventually, because of the baby boom after the war, higher standards of living and rising levels of pay for younger workers became a dominant factor of the economy. The Youth Revolution had arrived. People discarded the dowdy colours of the previous decades and began to discover and adopt fashion trends that often surprised their grandparents. New national names in retailing came to Romford such as C & A in the market place. Some old local retailers went out of business and other declined. In the late 1960s and early 1970s Romford's new shopping centre (Liberty One) and ring road became a reality. So did Gamages and (a sign of the times) Habitat. In the late 1960s there were still many smaller local cafés and restaurants including a relic of the 1930s opposite the Odean Cinema, a 'Milk Bar'. Gradually over the next decades these were squeezed out by fast food chain restaurants and, in the late 1980s and throughout the 1990s, by many new licensed premises and night clubs as social habits changed. The coffee bar revolution earlier in the 1950s and 1960s was of minor importance in Romford compared to the recent accumulation of modern style pubs, bars and recently real coffee establishments. A new variant that raised its flag in South Street in the last decade was an Internet Café. Two of the three older cinemas have closed, only the ABC remaining as a triple-screen cinema. A new multiple-screen cinema has replaced the old Odeon in South Street. This is located at the top of the Liberty Two complex. There are now a large number of night clubs in the town, spearheaded by the opening of 'Hollywood' in the 1980s.

Romford's attempt to reshape itself to allow for public transport needs as well as those of the car has resulted in a number of large multi-storey car parks and and the pedestrianisation of parts of South Street and the market place.

Millions of pounds have been spent in all these leisure, transport and shopping facilities and a continuing battle will be fought into the twenty-first century to enable the town to cope with fast changing lifestyles.

These solid Victorian houses stood in Laurie Square – the Central Library now occupies the site.

# The Start of the Century

Mawney Road Baths, opened in 1900, were the pet project of Councillor Craig who campaigned tirelessly to get them built. Although, for this reason at first they were known as Craig's Folly, they were a very popular and successful addition to the Edwardian town's amenities. In winter the swimming bath was boarded over and meetings and entertainments took place here.

Romford, *c.* 1909, approaching Western Road, in South Street. Note the early 10 mph speed limit sign. Before the shops came, private houses were predominant in this section which is now dominated by drinking places with tables on the pavement. Just beyond the young lad on the right is an old-style milk delivery cart waiting in the curb.

South Street, going further north towards the Golden Lion, was the beginning of the shopping area in 1904. This narrow section above Western Road was gradually widened between the two world wars.

The old earth bank on which the railway ran through Romford towers above the scene in 1902. The bank is no longer visible today. The horse-cab taxis await the arrival of a train and the passengers who will stream down the slope behind the white railings on their way from the station platforms.

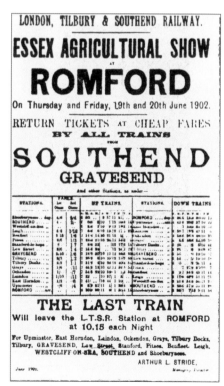

The London Tilbury and Southend Railway built a new line from Upminster to Romford in 1893, linking to the Grays–Upminster branch. There was a station between the Rising Sun Inn (now the Morland Arms) and the railway bridge. This poster advertises fares and the time of trains to the Essex Show which was held on the Marshalls Estate fields in June 1902. The Essex Show took place in Romford on a number of occasions before houses were built over the Marshalls fields from 1924.

21

J.P. Mackie's dairy milk float, 1911. The dairy was at 5 Park Lane where the fields stretched to Hornchurch in the first three decades of the century. Many dairy firms competed for trade in the rapidly expanding town.

A busy corner by the Golden Lion in 1906 looking up the High Street. Lasham's chemists and barber shop on the left had been founded in the nineteenth century in an old pub building that stood on this South Street corner. The shop was rebuilt as a fine commercial premises, but was shortly to be taken over by the legendary 'Tommy' England who became a property dealer and amateur planner as well as councillor. He was behind the Rise Park development and many others in the 1920s and 1930s. He also donated the parkland at Rise Park to the town as well as other land to various charitable causes.

The little fishers with their minders in a horse-drawn boat are taking a rest in the carnival procession at the top end of Romford market in the early 1900s. Their 'take' was almost certainly destined for the Victoria Cottage Hospital in Pettits Lane which, like most other cottage hospitals, was heavily supported by the people of its catchment area.

Romford Passive Resisters' Meeting in front of St Edward's Church, 11 September 1903.

The Resisters' sale of goods at the Police Station Yard on the same day.

In early September 1904 a report went round the town that a large number of valuable coins had been discovered in some rubbish in the High Street. Workmen who were making alterations to Cakebread's Grocery had to take up the floor. In the process they discovered rubbish underneath which they piled out in the street. The *Daily Graphic* of 8 September 1904 continues the story: 'While it lay there someone spied an old coin laying in it. He picked it up and began looking for more. His example was followed by several others, and soon a crowd were engaged in turning over the rubbish and searching for coins. Afterwards some tall stories of the finds were freely circulated. It was said that £200 had been extracted from the rubbish heap . . .'

Albion Street School lay hard by the railway embankment at the bottom of Queen Street. It had been built to serve the mid-nineteenth century New Romford estate of streets around it but the growing local school population demanded a bigger premises and, in 1896, the children were moved to the more commodious premises built in Mawney Road. Albion Street took over the infants' department of St Andrew's School which was also growing.

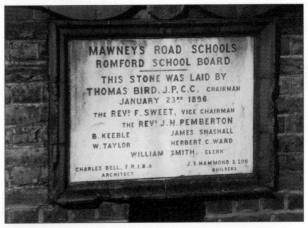

The Foundation stone of Mawney Road. It was quite a twentieth-century school incorporating various new ideas about education and much thought had evidently gone into the layout. It is possible that the Revd Pemberton was behind some of this. J.S. Hammond of Hill House, Main Road (where the DSS Office now stands) was responsible for much of the new building in Romford either side of 1900.

Mawney Road School, still looking quite new about 1906. The windows were designed to let as much light and air into the classroom as possible, although discipline was pretty strict in the early decades of the century.

On 22 June 1911 schoolchildren from Romford lined up in front of the church and sang 'God Save the King' which no doubt allowed them to give vent to some of the repression they suffered in class. Here they are with a good proportion of the Romford population of the time and a conductor standing on a podium of boxes improvised for the event. England then was an extremely patriotic nation. In more recent times this patriotism mainly surfaces when we do well at sport.

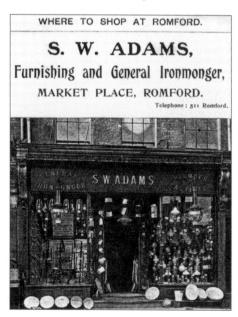

S.W. Adams took over the ironmongery business of Norman Halls in February 1900 and his shop was very well known in the district for seven decades. It closed its doors on 18 April 1970. It was said Adams' shop could produce every item of what would now be called 'do-it-yourself' equipment that anyone could ask for. Adams employed a large number of tradesmen to fit out the houses of the wealthier inhabitants. Their work included bell handing – they would frequently be asked to set up a system of bells in a house so that servants could be called to any room at a touch of the bellpush. Even quite small middle-class households would employ one or two servants before the Second World War.

This fine house 'Edfu' stood on the corner of Main Road and Junction Road. It was built in 1909 by a respected general practitioner, Harold Upward. The merit of building it on a corner was that there could be separate private and patient's entrances. Doctor Upward had his own small dispensary included. The house was the source of much admiration to Romfordians because of the very fine pointing between the brickwork.

Edward Upward, a son of Dr Harold Upward, is one of Romford's literary lions. Few people in the town know that he has played a great part in the history of twentieth-century English literature. He was once described as the 'fourth man' of a world-famous literary trio who have made news all over the globe – Auden, Isherwood and Spender. The three regarded Upward as their literary mentor but he has not perhaps gained the credit due to him. Surviving all three, he now lives in the Isle of Wight. In his nineties, he has gained more recognition with the re-publication of his experimental novels in recent years. Included among his works are *Journey to the Border*, *The Railway Accident and Other Stories*, *The Night Walk and Other Stories* and *The Spiral Ascent*. Upward Court, a block of flats now built on the site of the above house, commemorates father and son and their achievements.

The new houses in Meadway, Gidea Park, 1912. The Gidea Park Garden Suburb was built as a showpiece development that would prove that practical and attractive houses could be constructed at a reasonable cost for the ordinary man in the street. Gidea Park Limited was created by a number of Liberal MPs and others to oversee the development of this unique site, shielded from the town of Romford on one side by Raphael Park and on the other by the golf course.

This lone house, which stands proudly in Risebridge Road, is part of the Gidea Park development. A brochure was published to give a detailed description of the houses in the development and the ideals behind them. Entitled *The Hundred Best Houses*, it contains the names of many celebrated architects of the early twentieth century. Today the 1911 exhibition houses are the objects of pilgrimage by students and designers. The Gidea Park Civic Society, a local group, works to preserve the ideals and practice of the founders today.

A subtle curve in Heath Park Road reveals the new Romford County High School building in 1912. The view was later restricted by the building of further houses on the grassy plot to the right. A new building for the County High School was built in Brentwood Road in 1935. The two buildings later came together as the Frances Bardsley upper and lower schools – named after an earlier dedicated headmistress.

The Mawney Institute Football Club, 1912 local cup and league winners. There was tremendous enthusiasm for Association Football in pre-1914 Romford. As a team sport it no doubt formed a good basis for military comradeship two years later when war broke out. How many of these young men survived the conflict?

Members of the Clarion Cycling Club at their Romford summer camp in 1912. The group was one of a number of Clarion clubs throughout England, inspired by new left-wing ideals. The headquarters of this group is now known to have been at Nazeing to the north-west of Romford.

Clarion Cycling Club members obviously enjoying themselves at the Romford camp in 1912. The town then boasted plenty of open fields round the immediate perimeter. Such groups prefigured the post-war breaking down of strict social taboos that were inherited from the Victorians.

In the 1900s Romford Brewery was a town within a town, employing several hundred workers in the brewing process and ancillary craftsmen making barrels and other items needed as well as draymen, clerks and engineers. Apparently the brewery hit a bad patch financially at this time and they were criticised for poor management. Cornell in his manuscript description of the town said that 'old and tried servants had been dismissed to make way for less competent men'. In January 1909 a crisis led to a receiver being called in to manage the business, both in Romford and at Burton.

The top of South Street in 1914. Just above the rear entrance to the White Hart Yard on the left are five shops opened in a line of old cottages. The middle one offers hair cutting, shaving and shampooing for men – a rival to similar facilities offered by Lasham's at the corner of the High Street. A notice proclaims that a chiropodist is in attendance here. On the right there is an alleyway through to 'Page and Metcalfe, Wheelwrights and General Smiths', who also appear to be agents for Napier Motors. Wheelwrights at this time were often presented with the job of straightening out damaged motor-car wheels.

This line of shops, South Street, *c.* 1902, appeared as part of the Edwardian commercial expansion and were built on the site of a vacant field known as the White Hart Hoppet. National shopping chains have already moved in (Sear Bros and Sainsburys).

It is hard to believe that Romford Hall, an impressive house with gates, sketched here in 1902, once stood in its own grounds off South Street opposite where Barclay's Bank is now. Marks & Spencer stands on part of the site. A previous house had been sited further back in these grounds. Known as Stewards, it was the manor house where the poet Francis Quarles was born.

Cattle and their drovers wait for the auctioneers to come round to them in 1908. On the other side of the highway running down the middle of the market place are some general stalls and the shops of Stones (local forerunner of Debenhams) and Humphrey's, a famous baker's and café.

The end of a quiet market day by St Edward's Church, *c.* 1902. The name 'Cock and Bell Inn' still appears on the front of Church House even though it had ceased to trade. Note the cast-iron gentlemens' lavatories with a lamppost behind; these were later rebuilt underground.

The east end of the market plain in 1904. Behind the sheep pens and a few head of cattle we can see the Bull Inn and Peck's the bootmakers. The upper storey of the Laurie Hall is occupied by the Romford Town Mission at this time.

A clever 'spieler' draws a crowd to his elaborate stall, *c.* 1905. The Windmill and Bells public house and Stones department store are on the far right in the background. The lamp on top of the McCarthy fountain can just be seen behind the crowd.

These cattle lined up along the railings on the north side of the market make an arresting sight, *c.* 1911. Romford market was the cattle sales centre for most of south-west Essex.

37

Whitmore's steam mills at the bottom of Victoria Road are a long-forgotten Romford industry. The steam mill was built in the middle of the last century to replace a windmill. This view of the steam mill in its latter days illustrates a part of Romford that altered drastically. The block of shops that replaced it in the 1930s bears the name 'Old Mill Parade'.

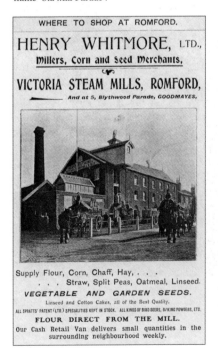

An advert for the Victoria Steam Mills showing them at the beginning of the century.

Another of Romford's treasures was the Victoria Cottage Hospital, seen here *c.* 1906. This was the facility that Romfordians generously contributed to at the various carnivals and fêtes of the early twentieth century. It served as a surgical unit for the town's general practitioners and was very proud of a fine medical record. The hospital was closed during the health cuts of recent years. Most of the buildings of the hospital, which gradually extended down to the bottom of Pettits Lane, are now in use as clinics of various kinds.

Merryweather's fire-engine being demonstrated at Romford Brewery, *c.* 1906. Ind Coope's were very conscious of fire hazards at their large premises which contained many wooden structures as well as thousands of wooden barrels, some of which can be seen behind the engine. The brewery fire-brigade staff operating the vehicle and its equipment are very proud of their significant role. On one or two occasions the brewery engine was called in to assist the town's horsed engines.

Waiting for the trains from London in 1904, cabmen and others stand easy before the evening rush hour. Some cabs wait in the yard between the station and the Star Inn. One cab on the left is parked at the end of Eastern Road which has been a cab rank for more modern taxis in recent times.

The High Street Romford is open for business on a typical day during the first decade of the century. The tall building in the centre of the photograph is the Coach and Bell Inn which had been rebuilt in 1895. W.J. Porritt on the left had both pawnbroker's and furniture dealer's in several premises which stretched round the corner to the left into 1 and 2 Mawneys Road as it was then called.

# A World in Conflict

Wilfred Owen, who became famous posthumously, is seen here *c.* 1917 after his graduation from the officer's training school at Hare Hall, Gidea Park. Owen produced some of the most telling poetry of the First World War, which reflected his growing disillusionment with what was going on in the deadly trench warfare in France. He was killed a week before the end of the war. Having twice been invalided out of the front line he could probably have escaped his fate but the 'officer' code instilled into him at the Artists Rifles training school at Gidea Park, plus his own inclination to 'be there' with his men, proved fatal.

The Barton-Rawson Airship in 1905. Before the war started, the British experimental airship (seen here) anticipated aerial warfare. The first stage of such warfare was dominated by the German 'Zeppelins'. Britain had lagged behind other great powers in developing aircraft. The early twentieth-century governments had ignored such projects and refused financial backing. Certain patriotic and brilliant inventors, however, were undeterred and carried on their experiments out of their own funds. Dr Barton, a medical practitioner, was one such inventor.

Mr Rawson steering the airship. Part of the frame is seen on a cart. The airship consisted of a gasbag 180 foot long and a deck made of bamboo poles 127 foot long with an engine giving an estimated 15.5 mph. The airship was constructed to try for the prize of £4,000 which the War Office had finally decided to offer for a craft capable of remaining airborne for three days with a crew of what was supposed to be three people. The brave aeronauts, the third and fourth of whom were Mr A.G. Gaudron and Henry Spencer (a well-known balloonist), rose from Alexandra Palace after 5 pm on 22 July 1905. The ship passed over Tottenham, Wanstead and Ilford, which it circled twice. A local journalist described the airship as the clipper of the clouds. Leaving Ilford the ship turned to Barkingside, the motors were stopped and the wind carried it in an easterly direction. Over Romford, Dr Barton decided it was time to descend.

A perfect landing was made on a potato patch within the grounds of Heaton Grange (now part of Harold Hill) where a garden party was in full swing. The problem was that, in the excitement of landing, the crew omitted to spread themselves on deck. They all stood at one end and the deck tipped up. They were forced to slash the canopy and release the gas to prevent the wind dragging the airship along the ground. One propellor was smashed and the stern motor ripped from its mountings. Thus ended the adventure. The two motors were salvaged but the remains of the airship were left for firewood and disposal.

St Edward's Hall on the east side of Laurie Square was home for the 'First Essex Royal Havering Volunteers', a predecessor of the territorial army, between about 1860 and 1870. The volunteers met here for drill and parades. Sergeant Major Courtney, the first drill instructor, lived in rooms over the top of the hall. In Park End Road during the nineteenth century was the drill hall and parade ground for another group – the No. 8 Battery, Essex Artillery Volunteers. There were many other groups of Volunteers in existence before the First World War. Indeed, Romford had a significant interest in military affairs well before 1914 when every school ground and other open area became a camp for newly recruited and regular soldiers.

When, in the month of August, 1914, Germany declared war upon civilization, the British Army numbered only 275,000. To-day it numbers considerably more than 5,000,000. From cottage and mansion, from office, factory and field, the men of Britain have flocked to the colours, and her sons from overseas have rallied, with a splendid spontaneity, to the common flag. Great Britain did not seek war, but, since war was forced upon her, she will not sheathe the sword till victory is secure.

(*Above*) Patriotic propaganda in the middle of the war gives details of the conflict.

This Romford market postcard from the First World War shows some soldiers in the background. They were part of the many thousands billetted around the town. Romford was a nearby source of entertainment in the brief respites allowed from army duties. An early silent film could be watched at the Laurie Cinema (a conversion of the old Laurie Hall) seen at the far end.

The Essex Special
Constabulary, Romford
Division, 1916. A call for
extra men to swell the
ranks in wartime was
made to those who were
not required for active
service.

The Main Road entrance to the Artists Rifles camp just beyond Hare Street hamlet, *c.* 1916, with sentries on guard.

Band practice outside a D Company hut. Every activity was highly organised within the camp.

Dedication of the Church Army hut at Hare Hall by the Bishop of Chelmsford in January 1916.

Balgores House, seen here *c.* 1917, was taken over by the Artists Rifles, as was Gidea Hall nearer Romford, to provide for the expansion of training demanded by the First World War's voracious appetite for officers and men to feed the guns in France.

47

This group of soldiers at Hare Hall appear to be lining up for rations. *c.* 1917.

A senior officer at Hare Hall camp poses for his photograph
*c.* 1917.

The canteen, c. 1917. An interesting view of the home comforts at the camp. These must later have been thought of as 'paradise' when the troops had been posted to the mud and carnage of Flanders.

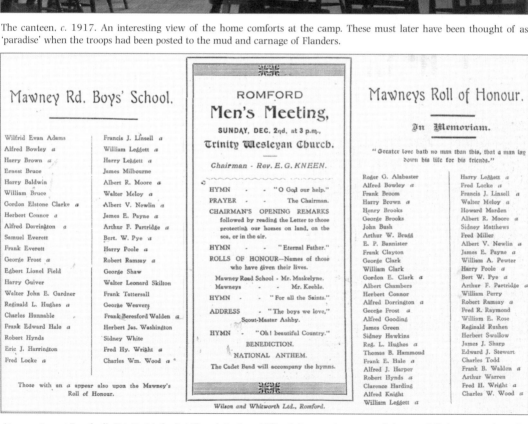

## Mawney Rd. Boys' School.

Wilfrid Evan Adams
Alfred Bowley *a*
Harry Brown *a*
Ernest Bruce
Harry Baldwin
William Bruce
Gordon Elstone Clarke *a*
Herbert Connor *a*
Alfred Dorrington *a*
Samuel Everett
Frank Everett
George Frost *a*
Egbert Lionel Field
Harry Guiver
Walter John E. Gardner
Reginald L. Hughes *a*
Charles Hunnable
Frank Edward Hale *a*
Robert Hynds
Eric J. Harrington
Fred Locke *a*

Francis J. Linsell *a*
William Leggett *a*
Harry Leggett *a*
James Milbourne
Albert R. Moore *a*
Walter Meloy *a*
Albert V. Newlin *a*
James E. Payne *a*
Arthur F. Partridge *a*
Bert. W. Pye *a*
Harry Poole *a*
Robert Ramsay *a*
George Shaw
Walter Leonard Skilton
Frank Tattersall
George Weavers
Frank Beresford Walden *a*
Herbert Jas. Washington
Sidney White
Fred Hy. Wright *a*
Charles Wm. Wood *a*

Those with an *a* appear also upon the Mawney's
Roll of Honour.

---

## ROMFORD
### Men's Meeting,
SUNDAY, DEC. 2nd, at 3 p.m.,
### Trinity Wesleyan Church.

Chairman - Rev. E. G. KNEEN.

HYMN     -   - "O God our help."
PRAYER  -   -   The Chairman.
CHAIRMAN'S OPENING REMARKS
followed by reading the Letter to those
protecting our homes on land, on the
sea, or in the air.
HYMN      -   - "Eternal Father."
ROLLS OF HONOUR—Names of those
who have given their lives.
Mawney Road School - Mr. Maskelyne.
Mawneys       -       Mr. Keeble.
HYMN   -   - "For all the Saints."
ADDRESS   - "The boys we love,"
Scout-Master Ashby.
HYMN   -   "Oh! beautiful Country."
BENEDICTION.
NATIONAL ANTHEM.
The Cadet Band will accompany the hymns.

Wilson and Whitworth Ltd., Romford.

---

## Mawneys Roll of Honour.

### In Memoriam.

" Greater love hath no man than this, that a man lay
down his life for his friends."

Roger G. Alabaster
Alfred Bowley *a*
Frank Broom
Harry Brown *a*
Henry Brooks
George Brooks
John Bush
Arthur W. Bragg
E. P. Bannister
Frank Clayton
George Clark
William Clark
Gordon E. Clark *a*
Albert Chambers
Herbert Connor
Alfred Dorrington *a*
George Frost *a*
Alfred Gooding
James Green
Sidney Hawkins
Reg. L. Hughes *a*
Thomas B. Hammond
Frank E. Hale *a*
Alfred J. Harper
Robert Hynds *a*
Clarence Harding
Alfred Knight
William Leggett *a*

Harry Leggett *a*
Fred Locke *a*
Francis J. Linsell *a*
Walter Meloy *a*
Howard Marden
Albert R. Moore *a*
Sidney Matthews
Fred Miller
Albert V. Newlin *a*
James E. Payne *a*
William A. Pewter
Harry Poole *a*
Bert W. Pye *a*
Arthur F. Partridge *a*
William Perry
Robert Ramsay *a*
Fred R. Raymond
William E. Rose
Reginald Rushen
Herbert Swallow
James J. Sharp
Edward J. Stewart
Charles Todd
Frank B. Walden *a*
Arthur Warren
Fred H. Wright *a*
Charles W. Wood *a*

At a meeting at Romford's Trinity Methodist Church in the middle of the war the names of the men killed in action from the local school and parish are honoured. Many more were to follow.

The County High School for Girls, Heath Park Road. On another postcard sent during the war a soldier, camped in the school outbuildings, has given his posting as 'B' company, 1st Cambridgeshire Regiment, E. Anglian Division. He writes to his lady friend: 'Thanks for the letter – will write later – no time at present 7–8 hours of drill daily. Have written to War Office for a Commission. We have neither pillows, beds or blankets but we use the floor and overcoats. Am living on bread, jam and corned beef. More later.'

Thousands of soldiers began their journey to the front from old Romford Station, *c.* 1914.

New motor taxis, *c.* 1914, available outside Romford station, were used by troops during leaves.

Part of Romford and District Detachment of the Essex Volunteer Regiment lined up in the park in the optimistic early days of the war.

51

Soldiers on trench-digging practice, *c.* 1916, somewhere near Gallows Corner, Romford, during the war.

This postcard was addressed to Private Ernest Edwards 28890, 1st Essex Nr 105683, Limburg am Lahn Hessen-Hassau, Deutschland, on 19 December 1917. It was sent to him with bread rations and bears the message, 'With our best wishes for Christmas and the New Year' (Copenhagen Bread Bureau). The British Red Cross organised this bread-making and packing establishment in Copenhagen during the war. The object was to send food items to captured British soldiers in German prisoner-of-war camps. Germany was short of food and the prisoners were obviously a low priority.

Dora Collier of Junction Road, Romford, helped nurse wounded soldiers at the Romford War Hospital, Oldchurch. This is her certificate of war service issued after the war by the Red Cross.

**PRICE TWOPENCE.**

# The GREAT WAR, 1914-1918.

## Romford Peace Celebration

Saturday, July 19th, 1919,
— IN —

# RAPHAEL PARK

and field adjoining, kindly lent by Mr. Mann.

*Chairman of Committee :* G. J. RICH, Esq., J.P.

*Hon. Treasurers :*

L. SELBY, Esq., L.C. W. & P. Bank.

W. K. JAMES, Esq., Lloyd's Bank.

M. B. LARKIN, Esq., Barclay's Bank.

Mrs. P. HAYDON-BACON has kindly promised to present the Prizes at 7 p.m.

Donations received by Hon. Treas. and Hon. Secs. up to publication of Programme :—

|  |  |  | £ | s. | d. |
|---|---|---|---|---|---|
| Mr. and Mrs. P. Haydon-Bacon | ... | ... | 10 | 10 | 0 |
| Mr. and Mrs. R. Franklin | ... | ... | 10 | 10 | 0 |
| Messrs. Ind, Coope & Co. | ... | ... | 10 | 10 | 0 |
| Mr. W. Bailey | ... | ... | 5 | 5 | 0 |
| Mr. T. England | ... | ... | 5 | 5 | 0 |
| Mr. G. J. Rich, J.P. | ... | ... | 5 | 5 | 0 |
| Mr. L. F. Stone | ... | ... | 5 | 5 | 0 |
| Mr. J. A. Craig | ... | ... | 3 | 3 | 0 |
| Mr. E. Pearsons | ... | ... | 3 | 3 | 0 |
| Mr. W. Poole, J.P. | ... | ... | 3 | 3 | 0 |
| Mr. A. R. Tuff | ... | ... | 3 | 3 | 0 |
| Mr. J. B. Arch | ... | ... | 2 | 2 | 0 |
| Mr. S. B. Bennett | ... | ... | 2 | 2 | 0 |
| Miss Clifton | ... | ... | 2 | 2 | 0 |
| Mr. J. J. Craig, J.P. | ... | ... | 2 | 2 | 0 |
| Mr. F. A. Fox | ... | ... | 2 | 2 | 0 |
| Messrs. Kemsleys | ... | ... | 2 | 2 | 0 |

Romford Peace Celebration, Saturday 19 July 1919 – programme of events in Raphael Park. The front cover has the beginning of a list of donations by local notables and business people. At 1 pm for residents over sixty-five there was a dinner. Later at 4 pm there was a children's tea party and older children ate at 5 pm. The Romford Town Band under bandmaster Dawkins (a policeman in the town) played from 2 to 10 pm. There was also a small fair with swings and galloping horses. The evening ended with a huge bonfire, after which the band played the national anthem.

A 1921 photograph showing the dedication of Romford War Memorial on its original site in Laurie Square. There had been much debate about its design. Notice the cinema posters on the side of the Laurie Hall and the spectators on the roof.

Another view, photographed from the roof of the Laurie Hall, showing the large crowd. A small group is standing in Swan Field at the back (later the site of the Town Hall).

# A Sense of
# Achievement

North Street, Romford changed slowly as the 1920s began. The gradual
appearance of facilities for the all-conquering motor vehicle is visible. Many
men and their families had been shaken out of the old ways by their
experience of war – attitudes had changed.

A standard three class at Squirrels Heath in 1926. The master may have been too young to have been involved in the First World War. Many children had lost their fathers, particularly during the later bloody battles of the conflict. Women now represented a larger proportion of the teaching profession.

A General bus outside Romford's second station entrance. The station frontage was later converted into shops and a café. The bus services in and around Romford expanded at a fast rate in the 1920s aided by the need for mobility in employment (working men did not have cars) and the desire to go farther afield than the immediate locality for weekends and half-day holidays and to visit relatives and places of interest.

This neat Imperial bus – a Dennis – was operated by one of the local independent bus companies from a base in Marlborough Road. The owner, A.E. Blane, ran his buses from Collier Row to Romford station and Upminster.

Romford High Street, c. 1921. Some motor cars are already in evidence. The High Street was to lose its prominence as a major shopping area during the 1920s and 1930s as South Street quickly advanced to the No. 1 spot with an increasing number of shops and eventually two shopping arcades.

Looking through the Romford station arch in the late 1920s. The London and North Eastern Railway is offering cheap day return fares to Ilford and Brentwood among other local destinations. The railway was handicapped by having only two running lines through Romford until the beginning of the 1930s when this old arch was taken down and two new girder bridges put up in a major widening scheme.

Bramble's haircutting and shaving saloon in quiet Victoria Road, decorated for the Romford Carnival of 1929. Next door is the laundry.

Mr Bassett mounted on his horse in a side street off Victoria Road, 1929. For many years he led the Carnival from here to parade through the town.

Romford High Street, *c.* 1924, with the very small Romford Arms pub on the left and Guymer's house furnishers on the right. A sign a little way along on the left says 'Wireless' and indicates an agent for the modern radio sets which could receive broadcasts from the new-fangled BBC. The BBC began broadcasting in 1922. The shop would no doubt recharge the heavy acid-filled 'accumulator' equipment which powered the sets in many homes. Carrying this equipment along the street to the shop when transmissions got weak was a delicate business.

1928. The five Romfordians who founded the new Romford Football Team at the end of the 1920s. Before its demise in 1978–80 it played in the Southern League and got close to claiming a place in the professional leagues. In 1948–9 it reached the Amateur Cup Final at Wembley – it lost by a disputed goal to Bromley, the winners. Left to right: Bert Weavers, Bill Durrant, Glyn Richard, Albert Smith and Fred Collett.

The march of the suburbs. Heath Park Road, from the corner of Salisbury Road in the late 1920s when there was a corner shop here.

A growing number of subscribers used Romford telephone exchange between the wars. At first only businesses thought it worth while to instal a telephone.

The inside of what is now the old exchange harks back to the inter-war period. Note the functional staircase and the survival of the obsolete relay technology arranged in banks and tiers.

There was plenty of new building between the wars – Kingsmead Mansions is a good example of the sophisticated style of apartment building put up near the centre of Romford but tucked away behind the shops.

A contrasting view of the south side of one of Romford's seventeenth-century houses, photographed in April 1933 in London Road.

After a hiatus of over twenty years a new area of development was created by Gidea Park Limited at the northern edge of the Garden Suburb. The Modern Homes Exhibition created new flat-roofed and balconied houses in the International style of the time. This house in Heath Drive is now being restored by its owners in a sympathetic manner worthy of what is now a listed building.

The Heath Drive house has an excellent feeling of privacy as the main windows and the sun balcony face the garden.

A sign of prosperity in Romford market in the late 1930s was the construction of new bank buildings such as that of the National Provincial on the corner of South Street (right) facing Lloyds Bank. Further along Romford Shopping Hall replaced older buildings to provide under-cover premises and pedestrian walks for a multitude of smaller traders. South Street was now becoming rather expensive and is occupied by the big national shops – hence the nickname, The Golden Mile.

Stallholders and customers mingle during a typical 1930s market day. There is even a beat policeman keeping an eye on things without the aid of a walkie-talkie.

Permanent waving for women's hair became big business and these delightful views of Lucille's Salon are intriguing. Both ladies and gents are catered for, although the word unisex had not been heard of.

LADIES' AND GENTS.' HAIRDRESSING

*Lucille*

Tel.—ROMFORD 1643.     92, Dagenham Road, Rush Green, ROMFORD

EUGÈNE  PERMANENT  WAVING

Ladies' Cubicles.          Gents.' Department.

# MARCONI
### THE ARISTOCRAT OF GOOD RADIO

*Outstanding value in 1938 Radio*
**Is the Marconiphone 557**

12½ GNS.
A.C. MAINS

or 3/6 Weekly

An exceptionally attractive six-valve all-wave superhet table grand for A.C. mains that provides world-wide reception for the connoisseur —— at every man's price. This outstanding instrument receives world's programmes on three wavebands from 16.5 to 2,000 metres with remarkable fidelity of reproduction.

*See and here them at :—*
# SMARTS RADIO
### 2a-2b, Quadrant Arcade, ROMFORD.
MARKET PLACE ENTRANCE.     Phone : ROMFORD 2800.

*Or at Romford's Ideal Home and Fashion Exhibition——Stand No. 9 and 10. September 18th to 25th.*

By 1937 radios that plugged into mains electricity were becoming the norm as a large number of Romford houses were now connected to the grid. Houses tended to have a limited number of sockets, often only one to a room. Even so the majority of housewives still cooked by gas.

65

The South Street entrance to the Quadrant Arcade today. The third of Romford's under-cover shopping areas, it housed a dance hall on the top floor when it was opened in September 1935. It was unusual in its dog-leg shape as it turned a bend and ran through to the market. The construction began at the South Street end. Completion of the Market Place exit was delayed while the details were negotiated. The dance hall continued up until recent times and many remember it as the Shannon.

A barricade of cattle vans surrounds the auction area at the east end of the market.

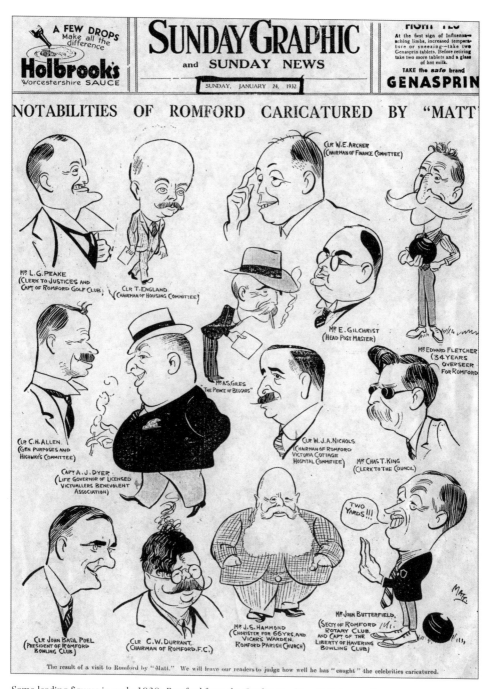

Some leading figures in early 1930s Romford from the *Sunday Graphic* artist's impressions.

A crane at work beyond Romford station digging out the path for two new lines of permanent way at the beginning of the 1930s.

Romford station from South Street and Eastern Road, 1999. When the track was doubled in the 1930s, the opportunity to rebuild the station was seized. From this angle it can be seen how the offices were built on to the side of the former embankment to blend in with Romford's other buildings.

In June 1936 the London and North Eastern Railway staged a Romford Railway Exhibition in the station yard and sidings. It was one of a series of public relations exercises held in various towns. There were a large number of exhibits representing all the aspects of railway operation. In this photograph a line of people are queuing to view the footplate of one of the most modern steam locomotives at the time.

Another huge attraction was the chance to ride in a wheel-less carriage hoisted into the air by a steam crane.

Another queue to look at the *Silver Fox* locomotive driving cab.

In 1937 Romford was granted Borough Status and with great foresight the new Town Hall was open in time for the ceremony. The building was designed to be economical but dignified and this brief was carried out with some flair. There are art deco features that would not have disgraced a cinema of the time. The building was recently listed as being of particular architectural interest.

Sir George Broadbridge the Lord Mayor of London came down to Romford to present the Borough Charter. Very often this job is carried out by a royal prince but 1937 was coronation year so the royal family was busy. The Lord Mayor deputised, putting on an excellent spectacle as he was accompanied by officials wearing period costume. He was driven from Gallows Corner in his historic coach which had been specially conveyed to Romford so that he could ride down Main Road to the Market Place.

Charles Allen as Charter Mayor with the Romford Borough Council members of 1937 in the foyer of the new Town Hall.

Various celebrations attended the granting of the Borough Charter. One event was the appearance of this old-time stage coach of the type that ran through Romford before the railway age.

Western Road College school photograph taken during the 1930s. This was a private school run by Edith and Grace Hammond.

Teachers at the Romford County High School during the 1930s.

Lunch break for the workmen building Havering Road School (now Parklands) in 1931. The school was constructed for Essex County Council by A. Saunders & Son.

Evans Corner, Rush Green Road, Romford, 1930. These shops and the houses nearby were erected by P.H. Evans, a local builder and contractor. The houses in Dagenham Road were being offered new for between £535 and £585 in 1930. The shop on the corner was called Wadmore's. It was a tobacconists, post office, confectioners, newsagent, coach booking office and lending library. This corner was, in fact, almost self-sufficient in the 1930s. A post box, telephone box, weighing machine and a wide variety of other shops offering food and services can also be seen.

*For Luxury Travel.*

# GIDEA PARK COACHES
LTD.

ROMFORD **2777-2778**
LAINDON      -    **67**
INGREBOURNE **2336**

**Romford Coach Station,
London Rd., ROMFORD**

CAIMLER CARS FOR HIRE

Tours and Excursions to
all Seaside Resorts, Race
Meetings, Whipsnade &
Aldershot Tattoo.

**PRIVATE PARTIES
CATERED FOR.**

Gidea Park coaches were available for party outings to the seaside. From Evans Corner there were local General buses to Romford station on routes number 308, 123 and 175 (the latter route still runs today). You could also get to Aldgate by Hillman's Saloon Coaches service from Upminster. Later this service was taken over by the Green Line limited stop coaches.

On the way back from Rush Green towards Romford was Grenfell Corner which faced the Roneo works. Here was yet another area of local shops including a post office – and a hardware store.

# The Battle for Britain

Rescue and civil defence workers assess the damage to houses in Stanley Avenue after the parachute mine explosion of 21/22 September 1940. Seventeen houses were demolished in Stanley Avenue and Carlton Road and many hundreds were damaged.

Government Gas Mask for Civilians. Note the ease with which the mask is slipped over the head.

Self-adjusting straps hold the mask in position by gripping firmly across the top of the head and back of neck.

A front view of the mask which is designed with a minimum of weight. The eye screen allows of a wide field of vision.

Gas-mask drill. Before the Second World War and in the early days of the conflict the great fear of the authorities was that poison gas would be used by the enemy. There was a great insistence on carrying the mask with you in a little bag at all times. As the war progressed this fear receded in the face of many others and the rule was relaxed.

Petrol rationing started on the 23 September 1939 and this Romford motorist is filling up on the evening before.

The sleepsafe shelter. At the beginning of the war there was a big shortage of the Anderson garden shelter kits. This consisted of an arch of corrugated iron that was sunk into a trench and covered with earth, over a concrete floor. Householders below a certain income got theirs free – eventually. Others paid a small sum. A number of firms offered other types of protection – in this case a concrete arch type that could be erected indoors.

After the 'phoney war' of 1939–40, night raids began to occur with some frequency. These youngsters have discovered the wreckage of a German Heinkel bomber brought down on open ground in Romford on Saturday 24 August 1940.

In the late 1930s Romford Borough Council was fortunate to have in their employ some very able people such as Victor Appleby, pictured with the latest gadget of pre-war days – a Dictaphone. As a Borough Surveyor he partly overcame the shortage of shelters by designing a special Romford version – later known as the 'Appleby Dumpling' which resembled an igloo and undoubtedly saved a number of lives.

Some of the damage and devastation caused by the Stanley Avenue/Carlton Road parachute mine on the night of 21/22 September 1940. The huge crater was one of the largest seen in the district.

Following the Stanley Avenue incident a special hut was brought to the street. Victor Appleby and other staff dealt with war damage enquiries. They showed a real flair for coping with a difficult situation and offered expert advice where it was most needed. Within eight days all emergency repairs had been carried out.

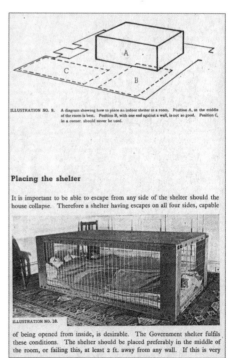

ILLUSTRATION NO. 9. A diagram showing how to place an indoor shelter in a room. Position A, in the middle of the room is best. Position B, with one end against a wall, is not so good. Position C, in a corner, should never be used.

**Placing the shelter**

It is important to be able to escape from any side of the shelter should the house collapse. Therefore a shelter having escapes on all four sides, capable

Another type of government-issue shelter was the Morrison pattern. These shelters were issued free to eligible householders in vulnerable areas. This shelter was meant to be used indoors and consisted of a box frame inside which the householder could sleep on a spring mattress. There were steel mesh sides. During the daytime the shelter could be used as a table.

ILLUSTRATION NO. 10.

of being opened from inside, is desirable. The Government shelter fulfils these conditions. The shelter should be placed preferably in the middle of the room, or failing this, at least 2 ft. away from any wall. If this is very

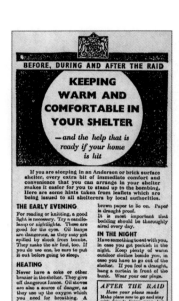

**BEFORE, DURING AND AFTER THE RAID**

## KEEPING WARM AND COMFORTABLE IN YOUR SHELTER

*—and the help that is ready if your home is hit*

If you are sleeping in an Anderson or brick surface shelter, every extra bit of immediate comfort and convenience that you can arrange in your shelter makes it easier for you to stand up to the bombing. Here are some hints taken from leaflets which are being issued to all shelterers by local authorities.

**THE EARLY EVENING**

For reading or knitting, a good light is necessary. Try a candle-lamp or nightlights. These are good for the eyes. Oil lamps are dangerous, as they may get spilled by shock from bombs. They make the air foul, too. If you do use one, be sure to put it out before going to sleep.

**HEATING**

Never have a coke or other brazier in the shelter. They give off dangerous fumes. Oil stoves are also a source of danger, as they use up the oxygen which you need for breathing. A candle heater is useful. Put the candle in a flowerpot, and then put a second flowerpot over the top. Raise the lower pot slightly from the ground. Try a hot water bottle or a hot brick in the bed. Heat the brick in the oven for two hours first and wrap it up.

**GETTING TO SLEEP**

A warm drink helps, particularly with children. Remember that when you are not sleeping on a thick mattress you need as much underneath you as on top. Have a good thick layer of newspapers or

brown paper to lie on. Paper is draught proof.

It is most important that bedding should be thoroughly aired every day.

**IN THE NIGHT**

Have something to eat with you, in case you get peckish in the night. Keep plenty of warm outdoor clothes beside you, in case you have to go out of the shelter. If you feel a draught, hang a curtain in front of the bunk. Wear your ear plugs.

*AFTER THE RAID*

**Have your plans made**

Make plans now to go and stay with friends living near, but not too near, in case your house is destroyed. They should also arrange now to come to you if their home is knocked out. It's comforting to feel that everything is fixed up, just in case.

**Help is ready**

If your home is damaged, there is a great deal of help ready for you. Full arrangements have been made to give you food and shelter, clothes and money if necessary, and to find you somewhere to live. If you have not been able to make arrangements with friends, go straight to the emergency Rest Centre. The wardens and police know where it is. *Ask them.*

**ISSUED BY THE MINISTRY OF HOME SECURITY**

A Ministry of Home Security notice published widely in Romford gave advice about shelter tactics. Many Romfordians had very solid large tables made of wood in their living rooms. While these did not give as much protection as Morrison shelters, they served as a substitute. One rescue worker extricated a lady from under such a table in her collapsed house by sawing through the leg of the table. He saved her life, but was then faced with a complaint that the rescue had ruined her furniture!

Only the frame survives of Henry Haysom's furniture shop in North Street after enemy raiders had dropped a high-explosive bomb in October 1940.

Romford Brewery buildings were blasted by a mine that fell at the rear on Exchange Street on 8 December 1940. In front are structures of the White Hart Yard which housed a blacksmith and motor coaches. The blacksmith's anvil was blown right over the rooftops into a shelter on the other side of the High Street. A body was thrown up on to the telephone wires and had to be cut down. In addition part of the telephone exchange building seen earlier in this book collapsed and had to be rebuilt.

What the Exchange Street bomb did to a car parked outside, 8 December 1940.

Tucked away in a side way off Heath Drive was this wartime sub fire station seen here with its staff. While the men are all listed with a surname and initials the lady is merely listed as Snowdrop – is this a surname or nickname?

This lady riding a horse in front of the Town Hall, *c.* 1943, was employed on a wartime drive to encourage investment in National Savings. The stunt was perhaps the idea of Mr Bassett who led the carnival procession on horseback.

Commander R.A. Ofstie, US Naval Air Attaché in London, paid a visit to Romford in February 1942 – probably in connection with some assistance given to US personnel, and signed the visitor's book in the Mayor's Parlour. He sits in the chair donated by the Rotary Club of Romford in 1937 while Mayor John Butterfield looks on.

A family's miraculous escape. During an air raid in September 1940, Mrs Kirk and her daughter were asleep on a mattress under the dining-room table, while her son slept nearby in an armchair. A huge bomb was dropped just 30 yards from their home. The house was wrecked but none of the three occupants were hurt. Mrs Kirk points to the mattress on which she slept and Mr Kirk is holding part of the chair which was demolished.

Copsey's Shop in the Market Place on VJ night, 1945. At this time shopkeepers celebrated the end of hostilities by lighting up their premises.

A children's peace party at the Wykeham Hall, 1945.

Military and civic leaders march on to the field at Romford Stadium on Saturday 20 September 1947 for a drumhead service and parade. The Borough of Romford honoured the Essex Regiment in this way.

The regiment and band with their drums marched ceremonially from the Stadium in London Road via the High Street, Market Place and Main Road to Raphael Park past a saluting base at the Town Hall forecourt. The regiment had been granted 'the Privilege, Honour and Distinction' of marching through the Borough on all ceremonial occasions with bayonets fixed, colours flying, drums beating and bands playing.

Variety and choice
– Romford market on
an ordinary day in the
1950s.

Musical chairs – the
last ones 'in'. Dee Way
coronation party, 6 June
1953.

The Lord Lieutenant of Essex officially opening the Romford War Memorial Old Folk's Club building, 21a Eastern Road, Romford, 11 October 1953.

Romford's Civil Defence ladies on a visit to the Houses of Parliament in November 1955. With them is MP Ron Ledger, who had won the seat at the election that year.

# The Colourful Decades

The new Romford Central Library was designed originally as part of the
County Library Service and many unusual features were installed. When it
was realised that Romford was to become part of a new London borough
some small modifications were incorporated. It is seen here as a new
building in 1965 when Laurie Square still remained around it.

Looking rather forlorn, *c.* 1966, the market superintendant's office of the time. This was housed in what remained of an old block of buildings which stood on the foundations of the 'new' market area that dated from the seventeenth century. It had been laid out over the site of an old tannery that was abandoned. These were the last days of this building and also of the tall Victorian houses in Laurie Square which can just be glimpsed at the back. These were demolished to make way for the ring road.

Facing Laurie Square in 1966 were these twentieth-century shops created out of houses from the Victorian era. They were officially part of the Market Place. The Dolphin Leisure Centre and widened roadway occupy the site today.

Castle's the printers, east of Church House, was an old-established Romford market family business up until the 1960s. The new vehicle entrance and exit to the Market Place were constructed in this area when the ends of the market were closed off.

This Victorian block faced on to the market, west of the Pig in the Pound pub up to the end of the 1960s. An extension to the Romford Shopping Hall replaced it.

East of The Bull pub on the south side of the market, Pearsons the jewellers was another long-established local firm. The temporary premises of the Westminster Bank was a site later used by other concerns while their permanent premises were erected or refurbished.

Brent & Collins became one of the men's fashion boutiques of the 1960s and 1970s, supplying the Romford male with fashionable clothes. This part of the market frontage has been extensively rebuilt in the last decade.

Caxton's bookshop was located in an old Georgian buiding, once a house. The building had several features dating from its origin including an unusually tortuous winding staircase. Caxton's final premises were in North Street near to the roundabout. A second bookshop was Wings in Arcade Place. Nowadays most of the books in Romford are sold through W.H. Smith in Liberty One.

The Congregational Church in South Street, seen here in the 1960s, was a landmark for seven decades of the twentieth century. Behind were the halls known as the Carlisle Institute. The modern church, now the United Reformed Church, is located in Western Road.

The traffic lights at the western end of the market regulate the traffic passing through. This scene has many points of interest for a student of twentieth-century changes in the town. At the very end of the 1960s the plan to re-route the traffic around the centre finally came to fruition.

The Market Place in the 1960s. Many of the old public clocks in Romford have now disappeared like the one in the photograph and the one on the Romford Shopping Hall. A new breed of clocks financed by advertising were set up at key points in the 1990s.

An antique bicycle in the Market Place, late 1960s. Victorian costume was donned to celebrate the end of an era. For a couple of years work had been going on to carve out a new ring road avoiding the market. Now the great day had come to say goodbye to the old route and welcome the new.

On the same day the barriers go across as the spectators relish their part in witnessing a piece of history. The old highway through the market that had existed for longer than the market itself was no more.

The members of Romford Council, 1963. They are already aware that the borough's days are numbered. Even the centuries-old office of alderman would be abolished, along with its distinctive gown which some of the members are wearing. Romford Council had long planned road and shopping developments for the town. These would be ushered in by a new authority the London Borough of Havering which would assume power on 1 April 1965. Also seen in this picture is the unique portmanteau desk and seating arrangements which were to be destroyed in the 1990s.

The Swan Inn building in its later days, dwarfed by Stones department store which has risen over it. The 1960s were a strange time in Romford when relics of the past were juxtaposed with the glaringly new. The Swan site is now the pedestrian thoroughfare – Swan Walk. Stones has become Debenhams.

The Double Diamond brewery as it was in 1969 looking north from the car park. Although this looks up to date, further extensive alterations to the premises were to be made in 1980. In spite of all the money invested in these improvements the brewery was closed down after being in existence for 190 years. This seems a strange kind of economics.

St Mary's High School operated from behind this modest frontage in Western Road. There were more extensive buildings and grounds at the rear. Romfordians were familiar with sightings of nuns who taught here. Their black habits added an interesting element to the town landscape up to the 1970s.

Although this Charity School building dates back a couple of centuries, the public library service only began in 1930. After representations by the Rotary Club of Romford asking for the provision of a library, an agreement was eventually reached for Essex County Council, the responsible authority, to use the Charity School for this purpose. The Branch (later Borough) Librarian, Gordon Humby, was instrumental in founding the Romford and District Historical Society here in 1956.

The new Central Library was built in what was then Laurie Square and opened in 1965. The building won a Civic Design Award. Originally planned for county library use, it was transferred to the London Borough of Havering where it has been the headquarters of the library service and the Central Library.

Part of the old Police Station in South Street in its latter days. Dating from 1892, it replaced the old police office and cell in the Court House, Romford Market.

The new Police Station in Main Road, opened in December 1965. It became the district police headquarters which up until then had been located at East Ham.

W.H. Smith's bookstall area at Romford station. This had been a familiar friend to travellers from 1930 through to the mid-1970s.

The old booking office at Romford station, early 1976. The appearance was drab and facilities needed updating.

All change at Romford station: later in 1976 a new booking office was unveiled with more convenient arrangements for staff and customers.

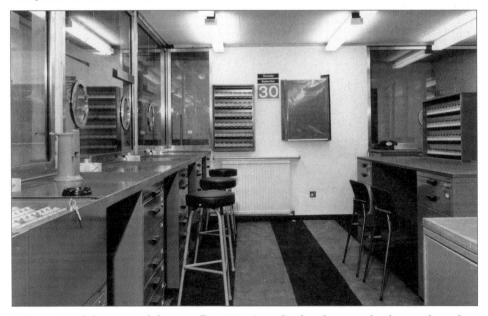

A closer view of the interior of the new office, 1976. Since this date the station has been modernised yet again and the booking facilities are now at first-floor level.

One of the most interesting features of the Liberty One Shopping Centre when it was opened was the installation of these plaques over the walkways. The plaques represent episodes of Havering's history.

Jimmy Savile, the well-known disc jockey, entertainer, fitness fanatic and charity fund-raiser met Judith Cottis and Hester Ardley when he visited Romford to host the 'Welcome to Citizenship' event at the Central Libary. This occasion was a response by the borough to the lowering of the voting age from twenty-one to eighteen and it took the form of a road show.

# *Looking Forward to the Future*

The entrance to Stewards Walk was altered after its first construction as part of Liberty One in the 1970s. This canopy and clock are part of a refurbishment for the 1990s. The highlighting of the entrance way reminds us that up to the 1960s this had been the entrance to the Gaumont (originally the Plaza) cinema, built in 1930 to replace the Victory further up South Street.

The Salvation Army Citadel rebuilt in the 1960s. One of the locations of architectural interest in Romford, it is seen here in 1999.

The Dolphin Centre awaiting further orders. This leisure pool, exhibition and conference facility made an interesting focus for the centre of Romford when it opened in 1981. However, maintenance costs, drastic cuts in local government and other problems have meant that it has remained closed for several years while a way forward is sought.

The extraordinary spiralling Havana car park access ramp is hidden away behind other buildings so that its visual impact is often only glimpsed – perhaps Romfordians were not ready for such architectural innovation.

Mercury House is a functional building that seems to have been intended to provide as much office space as possible. It is the K2 mountain at the far side of the original Liberty One development that now also looms over the Liberty Two complex built in the late 1980s. Visitors to the upper floors enjoy a wide panorama of Romford and its periphery.

109

A lost Romford landscape – this part of Park End Road between the Central Library and the back entrance gates of the Town Hall was in fact the total length of Park End Road until the rest was constructed from 1924 onwards. Before then a fence surrounded the Marshalls Park Estate north of this point and along the top of Church Lane. The buildings were demolished for the Town Hall extension and a car park in the mid to late 1980s.

The upper storey of this former doctor's house, one of the Victorian town houses that faced South Street, was still visible in 1988. This is a side view from Western Road. A shop had been built across the front garden and other commercial premises used the Western Road flank. The house disappeared in the 1990s to make way for new premises to house Yate's Wine Lodge, part of the 'Costa del South Street'.

This Victorian group of buildings in London Road has an interesting archway leading to a cobbled yard where a horse and cart would once have been accommodated. They were in the area of the former barrack block dating from Napoleonic times, part of which survived into the twentieth century. The site of this group now forms an extension to Allen's car showroom.

The offices of the old Romford workhouse of 1839 are still standing at the time of writing, but the building is under threat as the offices may move into a hospital on the other side of Oldchurch Road. These offices, together with the 'X'-shaped workhouse wards behind and the perimeter buildings of 1839, are part of Romford's heritage and it is hard to understand the reluctance of the national government department concerned to list them. They would make very suitable premises for a range of community uses. There is little enough left of the fine Victorian heritage that Romford once possessed. The twentieth century has seen much of that ruined by commercialism, leading to a less picturesque town. Tourists could still be attracted to what remains, and a workhouse would make an excellent museum.

The great hurricane of 1987 wreaked havoc among the trees of the borough which had been part of its attraction.

The fact that so many cars remained outside on the streets left them vulnerable to substantial damage during the hurricane.

Mawney Road-on-Sea. Considerable flooding has affected various areas near the River Rom in recent years and in fact throughout the century. This view in Mawney Road is an example.

Man-made upheaval. With the clearance of the old houses in Park End Road, a start could be made on the new extension to the Town Hall, July 1988.

Standing alone. During 1998/9 a strange landscape was created on the former Ind Coope brewery site. There is a substantial cleared open space but this solitary modern chimney remains.

The striking pattern of this external staircase in 1999 is the one impressive feature of the buildings on the site of the new telephone exchange.

The canopy of the 1930 platform buildings at Romford station seen from below in South Street in 1999.

In Victoria Road today a Victorian survivor can be recognised by looking at the upper floor of this fast-food premises. At the beginning of the century this was Whitmore's mill shop.

Cleaning up the river course. A feature of the 1980s and 1990s has been a consciousness of the environmental mess created by modern ways of living.

South Street bus-pull. Scenes like this have become more common as local people find ingenious ways to raise money for good causes, particularly in the last three decades of the century.

Helping Romford to celebrate 750 years of its official market, granted by King Henry III in 1247, are the Lord Mayor of London Sir Roger Cork (left) with the Mayor of Romford Del Smith. Behind are the Chief Executive Harold Tinworth and Leader of the Council Louise Sinclair. On the right is Air Commodore Brian Batt, Deputy Lieutenant with responsibility for the London Borough of Havering.

Another photograph of the anniversary celebrations of Romford market. Sir Roger Cork is seen with one of the Romford area's world-renowned youth bands. One of Sir Roger's predecessors as Lord Mayor had in 1937 presented Romford with its Borough Charter.

Romford café society, 1999. This building at the corner of Arcade Place and South Street was Romford's first shopping arcade opened in 1930 and converted to ordinary shops in the 1970s.

Jaks – another part of the 'Costa del South Street' leisure and pavement café area. It is housed in the former gas showrooms of 1937, later a financial institution office, on the corner of Eastern Road.

These lively relief figures of dancers and musicians are now displayed on the back wall of the Central Library. They were originally designed as part of the decor of the Dolphin Leisure Centre stairwell.

The Liberty Two shopping and leisure complex is furnished with escalators and lifts which operate in the atrium area of the centre. They provide a constant excitement of movement, colour, sound and contrast as visitors come and go.

A time capsule about to be buried. Many of these ceremonies have been performed in the 1990s in a revival of a practice popular in the first decades of the century. The capsules are often located under schools, churches and public buildings.

The staircase lift and clock tower were one of the earliest features of Liberty One when it was created and opened in the late 1960s and early 1970s. The foundation stone was fixed to the base of the tower to launch the project and in the 1990s a mosaic was added to the side to show creative activity by local people.

# Acknowledgements and Picture Credits

Kind thanks for use of pictures to Mr K. Langridge, London Borough of Havering, Mr S. Madell, Mr D. Partridge.

Particular thanks to Roy Squire for his archive and reproduction facilities.

Also grateful thanks to Brian Rider for excellent photographs of modern Romford.

Thanks also for assistance to Sue Smith and Tessa Sleat.